# The Prestige Series

# Ledgard

## A Reminiscence

## Mike Lockyer & John Banks

© 2004 M H Lockyer & J M Banks

ISBN 1 898432 98 8

*Front cover:* Wellington Street, Leeds, was not a bad place to watch the vehicles of the West Riding operators in the nineteen-sixties. In this August 1963 view near the coach station, Ledgard's 1957 Daimler CVG6 **XUG 141**, a Burlingham-bodied 63-seater, passes a Leeds City Transport double-decker. In the background were vehicles from the fleets of various of the BET companies. *(John Banks Collection)*

*Back cover:* A private party organiser acting on the exhortation "Hire a Coach ! Travel by Ledgard" might well have been provided with a Burlingham Seagull-bodied AEC Reliance 41-seater (1955's **UUA 791** is illustrated on the poster), but in later years a second-hand vehicle would probably turn up, **DCN 831**, for example, a relatively rare combination of Picktree body on a Guy Arab LUF chassis. This 35-seater, seen at Otley depot in May 1963, was one of eight similar 1954 machines to join the Ledgard fleet in 1963 that had been new to Northern General *(see page 52).* *(M H Lockyer)*

*Title page:* Samuel Ledgard soon saw the potential of Rackham's Leyland Titan and no later than 1930 was putting a batch of four into service. UB 2386-9 were all bodied by Leyland as lowbridge 48-seaters and **UB 2387** is illustrated in City Square, Leeds, in June 1932. *(John Banks Collection)*

*Opposite page:* Following Samuel Ledgard's death in 1952, his executors continued the business but were obliged to buy the majority of their vehicles second-hand. A typical example, and one that was familiar in the fleet from earlier new purchases of mechanically similar vehicles, was **EUH 959**, a 1950 Leyland Titan PD2 that had been new to Samuel Eynon, of Trimsaran. Ledgard's new PD2s had been highbridge, whereas EUH 959 had lowbridge 53-seat bodywork, also by Leyland. It was photographed in Otley bus station in the murk of December 1963. The Ledgard script in its prewar format is shown on the rear panels of **UA 2315**, a 1928 Dennis G 20-seater with Dennis bodywork, acquired from F Rathmell in 1936. *(M H Lockyer; Philip Battersby Collection)*

*Below:* A brief flirtation with Foden chassis in 1949-51 culminated in this fine Plaxton-bodied PVSC 37-seat coach, seen when brand new with the fantasy registration **FWP 1951** (Mr Plaxton's initials and the year). It would be registered ONW 2 for Ledgard service *(see page 28).* The rear wheel covers were not to survive the rough and tumble of daily use. *(John Banks Collection)*

# INTRODUCTION

## *"Sammy" - A Reminiscence*

Samuel Ledgard was often referred to as "Sammy", but never to his face; his intimates knew him as "Sam" and he was more than merely a bus operator, although he was one of the pioneers. He was first and foremost a businessman, and one of many talents.

Born in 1874, in his early twenties he took over the licence of the Nelson Hotel, Armley, Leeds under lease from his father in 1897. In 1900 the hotel was willed to Sam. The hotel survives and now bears a blue plaque in memory of the man.

Apart from the hotel, Ledgard eventually owned a brewery and a bottling plant. In the latter he bottled his own brew as well as ales for other manufacturers, such as Guinness and Bass.

Sam then branched out into the hiring of marquees and outside catering, which meant that transport was required. These ventures were not everyday happenings so he undertook haulage work, initially with horses and later with steam wagons. The first steamer was a second-hand Coulthard, bought in 1906. As the dawn of motoring began to change into full daylight, Ledgard leased the Bridge Garage from its founders and was thus equipped to service and repair his own vehicles as well as to take in outside work.

As if all that were not enough, he was also a cattle dealer, buying much of his stock from Wales and Ireland; his purchases had a short life expectancy, most of them passing through the Leeds abattoirs.

Later Ledgard turned to quarrying and gravel extraction and, later still, to farming, but in the meantime he became one of Yorkshire's best-known passenger transport operators, fitting his petrol-engined lorries with demountable charabanc bodies for weekend trips to the coast and to race meetings, at which he no doubt supplied the refreshments.

He also bought quite a lot of the property adjacent to The Nelson, partly as investment and partly to extend his brewery. This was a wise move because, although he did not sell much of it, it later provided space for the Armley garage.

The first Ledgard bus service started in 1924 as the result of taking over a small firm, the forerunner of many similar deals that took place in the years up to the outbreak of World War Two. Indeed, it is fair to say that most of Ledgard's stage carriage services were the result of buying out small, and one or two not so small, companies. As always with volumes in *The Prestige Series*, neither a fleet list nor a definitive history is being offered, but it may be mentioned that among the firms that succumbed to the lure of "Armley brass" were Ward of Horsforth (1924), Cream Bus of Burley-in-Wharfedale (1925), Barrett & Thornton of Otley (1927), Jules Antichem of Burley-in-Wharfedale (1927), Arthur Thornton of Otley (1933), Moorfield Bus Company of Yeadon (1934), B. & B. Tours Ltd of Bradford (1935), F Rathmell (1936) and G F Tate Ltd of Leeds (1943).

Among the ex-Antichem vehicles were some AECs, but Sam was primarily a Leyland man and he bought many chassis, through a Leeds agent, over the years. He did try other makes, notable Albion, ADC, Daimler, Dennis and Maudslay, but only in small, or single, numbers, and always went back to Leyland, ordering a total of 104 of the Lancashire firm's models, often in batches of four.

What would he have ordered today, one wonders?

What of Samuel the man? Quiet, with a reputation for being "careful", which in Yorkshire means exactly that, and not to be confused with "meanness"; he was at times extremely generous.

I used sometimes to see him watching his buses at the King Street terminus in Leeds, and wondered who the man in the grey tweed suit and flat 'at was. I asked a conductor once, who said: "Doesn't tha' know who he is? 'E be Sammy Ledgard." He pronounced the name "Leggard" as was sometimes done in Leeds. After that, I sometimes bid him "good-day", receiving a grunt and a nod in return.

He looked for loyalty from his staff and was loyal in return; those who were not loyal did not stay long with the firm.

His crews were a motley lot in the early days. Uniforms evolved gradually: from 1932 there were white coats and peaked caps for coachmen, and new blue serge coats, with

"Ledgard" on the lapels, for winter use. Light-blue summer jackets were issued in the fifties.

Samuel hated the rival West Yorkshire Road Car Company, which, like him, had built up its business through takeovers of competitors. Apparently West Yorkshire made an offer to Sam in the early 1930s, asking him, in effect, how much he wanted for his business. The story goes that he scratched his head and said: "Nay, lad, ah doant really know, like. Tell thee what, 'ow much will'st tha' tek for thine?" Apocryphal? Well, yes, and the story was subsequently corrected by Sam's son: it's a shame to allow the truth to spoil such a lovely cameo of the man, but I do not doubt that it is absolutely typical of Sam.

Samuel's buses were always notably faster than the rival West Yorkshire ones, and when WY bought their first Leyland TD1 Titans, with outside staircases, he promptly, doubtless with a sly smile, ordered double-deckers with enclosed stairs.

He was insistent upon good timekeeping. My father was a driver at Armley up to the outbreak of World War Two; one day when reporting for duty he was told that the boss wanted to see him. He went into the office and, without preamble, Sam said to him: "Tha' left Glenroyal a minute and 'alf early yesterday. What's ta' say, lad?" My father explained that he had gone by his watch, but maybe it was a bit fast… Sam's reply was; "Nay, that won't do, lad. Ah'm givin' thee two days suspension an' if it 'appens agen it's 't sack." Father, realising that argument would make things worse, turned to leave. As he was opening the door Sam added: "And whilst tha's off, lad, buy thissen a decent watch."

Such summary action was typical of Sam; very few members of staff held grudges apart from the few "fiddlers" who, when caught, were dismissed on the spot and knew that their chances of any further employment in the same area, much less another job conducting on buses, were remote. Although many regarded bus conducting as a menial job, one had to have a spotless personal record to become one. Even a fine for riding a bike without lights was regarded as a stain on one's character.

Samuel Ledgard died on Friday, 4th April 1952. In view of his well-known business acumen, it is all the more surprising that Samuel left a confused situation behind him, the effects of which were drastic. Such business activities as the catering, tenting and brewing had never been officially wound up after their discontinuance at the start of the war, and were deemed to be still in operation. Thus, death duties were charged on the whole estate. Coupled with this potential disaster were the start of the decline in postwar bus travel and an urgent need for new rolling stock and there is small wonder that "closing down" rumours abounded. One minor result of such tales was the author's commencing the then almost unheard of activity of bus photography in an attempt to keep some sort of record. Many of the pictures in this book were taken as a direct result of that situation.

It was, however, the start of a new and fascinating era, in which no fewer than 172 buses were bought second-hand, as against seven new ones and six new coaches, and this is not taking into account some that were bought only for spares. Out of it all arose one of the most fascinating and absorbing bus companies; in 1962, for instance, the fleet contained examples of AEC Reliance and Regent V, Albion, Atkinson, Bedford, Bristol K6A and K6B, Daimler CWA, CWD, CVD and CVG6, Foden, Guy, Leyland PS1, PS2, PSU, PSUC, PD1 and PD2 and Maudslay. At the end, ex-London Transport RTs were in the majority.

It is a matter of regret that the new régime did not keep any of the original buses. The preservation movement was some years in the future and all the early vehicles Samuel had kept (he rarely disposed of time-expired units) went for scrap in the months following his death - Caledon, Karrier, Leylands… A redeeming feature of these disposals was that they raised the cash to purchase 23 ex-London Transport Daimler CWA6s, thus keeping the blue wheels rolling.

The end was sudden. An announcement in August 1967 explained that terms had been agreed with the West Yorkshire Road Car Company for the sale of the business, which took place on 14th October of that year. What Samuel would have thought of this is hard (or perhaps all too easy) to imagine. He would have preferred his company to go to almost anybody else, even Leeds Corporation, for whom he had no love.

I now live many miles from where the blue buses once roamed, but on my visits to their erstwhile haunts the memories are strong, and I shall retain them to the end of my days.

As good a memorial to "Sammy" as any might be that, despite his opposition to trade unionism, there was very little industrial action taken in his lifetime, although in the 1957 national provincial bus strike Ledgard crews were to some extent involved. Following the takeover, there was a one-day strike on 7th October 1967, in protest at some of the working conditions imposed by West Yorkshire. WY crews used this as an excuse not to operate in Ledgard territory for the day in the Otley area - the protest was mainly by Otley depot staff.

## Ledgard Services

Routes operated were as follows:

> Leeds - Ilkley via Guiseley.
> Leeds - Ilkley via Otley.
> Leeds - Bradford via Pudsey.
> Pudsey - Calverley.
> Leeds - Horsforth via Hawksworth Road.
> Otley - Arthington.
> Otley bus station - Weston Estate.
> Otley - Newall - Otley.
> Otley - Horsforth via White Cross.
> Otley - Horsforth via West Chevin.
> Otley - Ilkley.
> Ilkley - Middleton Sanatorium.
> Bradford - Harrogate via Otley.

This last shared Harrogate bus station with the battalions of West Yorkshire. Far from it being a case of "come into my parlour", I think that Sam saw it as a case of invading West Yorkshire territory: he was always looking for ways to irritate them. It is said that he bought B. & B. Tours, who operated this route, for this very reason, made all the more piquant because West Yorkshire had bought out the predecessors, Blyth & Berwick; but Blyth & Berwick started up again as B. & B. (1928) Ltd and then sold out to Samuel.

There was a timetable of sorts for these services: 16 pages of typescript, using different typewriters and then hand duplicated. I think it cost 3d in old money (about 1p today, but that is not allowing for inflation).

## Tickets

The most common tickets were the ordinary Bell Punch. The tickets, perforated in the middle from 1½d upwards, started from ½d. An exchange ticket was issued on a return journey.

Cream Bus tickets were white with a blue heading and when taken over by Ledgard the system was continued, the tickets being altered with the wording "Ledgard's Blue Buses". As far as I know these were used only from Ilkley depot.

B. & B. used the Willebrew system: cumbersome but well-nigh foolproof and tamperproof. Tickets were white for singles, and returns were green. A purple exchange ticket was given when the green was surrendered.

Ultimate tickets were used on Otley local journeys up to 1965 when they were replaced with Setrights.

B. & B. discontinued the Willebrew system in the early 1950s when the usual Ledgard Bell Punch type was introduced, but instead of "Ledgard Services" printed vertically on the tickets, they bore the words "B. & B. Tours Ltd" printed horizontally on each half of the ticket. After the death of the founder, when the companies were reconstituted, this was changed to "S. Ledgard (Bradford), Ltd."

Finally, in 1955, the Setright Speed machine was introduced, largely - it must be said - to counteract the "fiddling" that was then rife, and this machine was in use until the end. Indeed, the ticket machines were taken over by West Yorkshire and for several years the machine number on a ticket was often an SL one.

## Liveries

The original livery was sky-blue with a white roof and a very large LEDGARD fleetname in gold on each side, complete with an indigo-blue waistband. A major variation was two Leyland PLSC Lions, which Samuel put into service in a red livery. When the first double-deckers arrived, the original livery was retained, but with a green roof. The latter was necessary because the roofs were of a fabric material and were treated with something closely akin to aircraft dope. This colour scheme was retained almost to the end of the 1950s. The colour split was sky-blue lower- and upper-deck panels, white lower- and upper-deck window frames and green roof. The rear dome was white on the TD1s, thereafter blue. After the war the blue was changed to Nile-blue (approximating to royal-blue) with the rest staying the same.

There were many variations of the blue theme after Sam's death, some described as "experimental liveries". The old colour scheme made a strong comeback, although the pillars were now blue and there was just one white band, between the decks.

Ledgard bought two coaches from Baxter, of Airdrie, which were two-tone blue, the lighter shade being almost a duck-egg blue. From about 1959 all buses adopted this shade, though the main colour of Nile blue remained the same. Until 1964 coaches generally had their own colours of Nile blue (before the buses were so painted) and a deep, buttery cream, with a black roof. From 1964 Ledgard used seasonal hire coaches from dealers, which were in stock colours of light blue and cream, after which Armley's own coaches were painted to match.

A variation was the B. & B. Tours vehicles, which retained their old colours of red, light blue and ivory until repainted in Ledgard livery in 1946/7.

## Depots

There were five depots. Armley, built by Samuel Ledgard, opened in 1932 and was well known for its unusual feature of the bus park being on the roof, necessary because the approach to it was down the short, steep Lamb Hill - continue past the front of the building, up the other side, turn right, through the gates, and you were on the roof. Ledgard's one steam cleaner was kept up there, together with a ramp for steam cleaning vehicles. The main paint shop was in the garage below. After the demise of the Company, Armley depot remained empty for some time and was eventually demolished to make way for a new road, appropriately named "Ledgard Way".

Otley depot was the second biggest. Much of the preparation of second-hand buses was done there, and a fair amount of painting as

well. Within shouting distance of Otley bus station, it is a corrugated metal and stone construction and is the only Ledgard depot still standing, although there are rumours of a new supermarket (well, it would be! - either that or a car park…) that will require its demolition.

Yeadon depot was inherited from the old Moorfield company. It was rebuilt in 1947 after the original structure collapsed in a gale. It was used after the end of the war as a dumping ground for old buses when the Armley rooftop bus park became too full. It was sold at auction in 1968 and the ground bought for housing development. Thus the depot was quickly demolished to make way for a small estate of new houses.

Ilkley was really an outstation to Otley and five service buses were stationed there. It was a one-piece, purpose-built depot with two pits. After sale in 1968 it was used by the local council to house refuse wagons and was later demolished. Houses were built on the site.

Bradford was a metal shed of somewhat peculiar construction, believed to have been built as an exhibition hall, with a metal framing and wire cross-bracing on each side. Like the others it was sold in 1968 and demolished.

One other building that still stands, albeit radically altered, is the old Cream Bus Service garage at Burley-in-Wharfedale, on the main road to Ilkley. This had been vacated in 1931 when buses allocated to it were transferred to Ilkley and Otley. It became a motor repair garage until about 1946/7 when it became a filling station and car sales pitch, later being used for car sales only. Today it is a motorhome sales site, and the casual observer would be hard pressed to discern anything of its Ledgard history.

*Mike Lockyer*
*Chippenham*
*May 2004*

### Editorial afterword and acknowledgements

To one not steeped in Ledgard lore from an early age the highlights stand out all the more. Perhaps the most striking is of a journey to Ilkley from London in the summer of 1961. I had been living and working in London only since 1st May of that year, and was still - indeed, am to this day - intoxicated with the wonder of London Transport and its vast fleet of identical RTs; most of them were, fittingly, on AEC chassis from "the builders of London's buses", but some had, if I may borrow my friend Brian Thackray's wonderful phrase, Lancastrian underpinnings.

On that journey to meet parents in Ilkley, I alighted from the train at Bradford and was directed to a bus stop. It seemed like home from home when a Ledgard RT turned up. Closer examination revealed that the vehicle, though smart, was perhaps not as well maintained in every department as its fellows still active in the Capital (Aldenham vs. Armley could have only one result...) and, of course, the blue livery was a bit of a jar after LT's red or green. In due season deposited in Ilkley for a brief break, I took a few photographs of Ledgard vehicles, and was soon on my way back south.

Mike Lockyer's lively reminiscences of the operator have served to reintroduce me to Ledgard and to fill in the gaps in my own recollections. And what a fascinating fleet it is to recollect. The late picture of hordes of ex-London vehicles takes no account of the rich diversity of non-London AECs, Albions, Atkinsons, Bristols, Daimlers, Fodens, Guys, a Maudslay, Ford and Bedford coaches and a fine selection of new or second-hand Leyland Titans. On page 63 of this book I suggest that the Ledgard fleet reminds one of that of Barton. Any large fleet using primarily second-hand vehicles, including a strong contingent of former London Transport machinery, is bound to do so. But in two respects Sammy differed from the celebrated Nottinghamshire operator - there were ECW-bodied Bristols in the fleet, and fleet numbers - so prominent on Barton's vehicles - were not used by Ledgard.

So, let us wallow in reminiscent mood (as far as we may within the confines of 64 pages) over a striking, sturdy, stalwart independent that held its own against the big guns and enlivened the West Riding scene for some decades.

Many of the photographs in this book were taken by Mike Lockyer, or are from his collection; I am also grateful to John Senior, Philip Battersby and Ron Maybray for their usual unstinting and much-appreciated help, and to Dave and Mary Shaw for reading the proofs. A special word of thanks this time to Don Bate and John Fozard and, as always, to the PSV Circle whose fleet history of Ledgard has been most helpful.

It has not been possible to illustrate every Ledgard vehicle, or even every batch, in the space available: for the prewar period in any case there are, as is usually the case, many vehicles that have not come our way in photographs; the postwar years are better represented but it would have been inappropriate to offer the reader page after page of identical RTs, RTLs and RLHs, fascinating and interesting as those fine vehicles are - indeed, there have been and no doubt will be complete books devoted to them - and a small sample only of Ledgard's ex-London Transport fleet has been allowed in here.

Readers are reminded that this book is an illustrated reminiscence: it makes no claim to be either a definitive history or a fleet list; to the reader anxious to know more about the legendary "Sammy", the book *Beer and Blue Buses*, written and published this year by Don Bate, is highly recommended.

*John Banks*
*Romiley, Cheshire*
*April 2004*

**Motor Chars-a-Bancs, Taxis, Motor Haulage.**

BENZOL,
PETROL,
OIL,
TYRES, &c.
AT
Lowest Price

ACCESSORIES
AND
REPAIRS.
✤
'Phone
3730.

**Bridge Garage, Lower Briggate, Leeds.**

THE MOTORIST'S RENDEZVOUS.     OPEN DAY & NIGHT·

*<< Opposite page:* Samuel himself at the wheel of a Karrier *char-à-bancs.*

*This page:* Another Karrier, **U 1949**, a Nicholson-bodied 29-seater, appeared on advertising postcards for Ledgard's Bridge Garage and Nelson Hotel.*(All: M H Lockyer Collection)*

For Steam or Petrol Motor Haulage, and Motor Char-a-Bancs———'Phone Central 3330.

QUOTATIONS SOLICITED FOR PARTIES

SAM<sup>L.</sup> LEDGARD, ARMLEY, LEEDS.

*Above:* A Karrier type PB70, **U 2706**, delivered in 1914 on private hire work at an unknown location. Those passengers who did not move while the photographer exposed his plate can be seen to be a grim-looking, unsmiling lot.

*Below:* Rackham-designed vehicles are the image of a successful Leyland Motors in the 1928-39 period, but the Lion was of pre-Rackham origin. It sold well and, with successive improvements, was available up to the outbreak of the Second World War. This PLSC3 version with Leyland 31-scat bodywork, **UA 4145**, was new in 1928 and withdrawn in 1936. It ended its days as a caravan. It was still very new when photographed in Station Road, Otley. *(Both: M H Lockyer Collection)*

*Above:* An earlier Leyland Lion, 1926's **UM 6696**, was a PLSC1 model (which had a shorter overall length than the PLSC3). In this idyllic scene at Grassington, probably in 1926 when the vehicle was brand new, it chanced to be in the picture when a vintage - even then - Renault, a Trojan and a horse-drawn cart were immortalised. Though not easy to spot, sister vehicle **UM 6697** is also - just - visible through the windows of UM 6696. The small bus ahead of the pair of Ledgard vehicles appears from the original print to be registered **WU 5488**. *(John Banks Collection)*

*Below:* As well as Lions, Tigers from the Leyland menagerie were bought, including six TS1s in 1931 as chassis only to be bodied in Ledgard's own workshops. Most of them seem to have been turned out for this private hire - clearly an important occasion. *(Ron Maybray Collection)*

# The Prewar Period

The first Ledgard Leyland Titan arrived in 1930, one of a batch of four with Leyland lowbridge 48-seat bodywork. **UA 2386** was withdrawn in 1943 but not disposed of until 1952 when it went for scrap to a Bradford dealer. These views date from April 1930 and show the gleaming vehicle before delivery to Ledgard. *(Both: John Banks Collection)*

*Above:* Here is Titan **UB 2386**, shortly after entering Ledgard service, at Wellington Street, Leeds. *(M H Lockyer Collection)*

*Below:* More TD1 Titans, with similar bodywork, came in 1931. **UB 5748** was one of a batch of four. It was photographed in City Square, Leeds, in June 1932. *(John Banks Collection)*

Daimlers were not common in the Ledgard fleet before the war, but in 1934 Samuel tried a CP6-type double-decker, with highbridge 54-seat bodywork by Charles Roberts. The vehicle, registered **UG 7252**, was an exhibit at the 1933 Commercial Motor Show, and was used as a demonstrator before starting work for Ledgard in March 1934. It was withdrawn in 1946 and sold for scrap in 1952. *(Both: Senior Transport Archive)*

*Above:* The Daimler CP6 double-decker was in competition with two Leyland Titan TD3 models also bought in 1934. Lowbridge 53-seaters, they were registered AUB 489-90. The first of them is shown when brand new. This was the first diesel-engined bus in the fleet. Both were rebodied (in 1938 and 1939) and withdrawn in 1953. *(M H Lockyer Collection)*

*Below:* The Leyland Cub appeared in the fleet in 1930. This one, **UB 5739**, was from the following year and had a Leyland 20-seat body. *(Ron Maybray Collection)*

*Above:* Perhaps the most exotic vehicle up to that time arrived in 1935. **CUB 1** was a Maudslay SF40 with a Brush centre-entrance coach body seating 36. It was exhibited at the 1935 Commercial Motor Show. Originally petrol-engined, it was in 1948 converted with a Leyland 8.6-litre diesel unit. It was withdrawn in 1951. Its body was rebuilt and fitted to an ex-London Transport Daimler chassis and its own chassis scrapped. *(Senior Transport Archive)*

*Below:* Rather more conventional in 1935 was a pair of Leyland Tiger TS7s with Leyland 33-seat rear-entrance coachwork. **BUA 403** was the second of them: seen here in postwar days with its original body, it was rebodied in 1953 and withdrawn in 1956. *(R F Mack)*

*Above:* In 1953, Leyland Tiger **BUA 403** was fitted with an Eastern Coach Works service bus body formerly carried by an East Yorkshire Motor Services Tiger TS8. After withdrawal the vehicle ran for a fairground showman from 1957 to 1961 and was then scrapped. *(R F Mack)*

*Below:* The other 1935 Tiger TS7 was **BUA 402**, which was also rebodied. This time a Barnaby bus body formerly carried by a Daimler COG5 in the fleet of Bullock, of Featherstone, was used. The rebodied combination lasted two years longer than did its sister, not being withdrawn until 1958. It was scrapped the following year. *(John Fozard Collection)*

**Upper:** Nineteen-thirty-five was also notable for a batch of three Leyland Titan TD4s, with Leyland lowbridge 53-seat bodywork. **BUA 400** was the middle one of the three, seen here in King Street, Leeds. All three had received new Leyland 52-seat lowbridge bodies in 1938. *(M H Lockyer Collection)*

**Centre:** One of the 1935 Leyland TD4s is seen with its original Leyland body when brand new. The two 1934 Ledgard TD3s and the trio of 1935 TD4s were all legally owned by Cream Bus and were built with vee-fronted Leyland metal-framed bodies, a specification that was then at the cutting edge of coachbuilding technology. The bodies were not successful, hence the early rebodying. *(Ron Maybray Collection)*

**Lower:** **CUG 843**, a 1936 Leyland Tiger TS7 with English Electric 32-seat front-entrance coachwork, was later reseated with 33 bus seats and withdrawn in 1956. *(John Fozard Collection)*

The Titan/Tiger progression continued in 1937 with a solitary TD4 lowbridge double-decker (EUG 123) and a quartet of Duple-bodied 32-seat coaches (EUG 124-7) on Tiger TS7 chassis. In the picture above **EUG 127** is shown during a 1937 tour by the Australian rugby team. Three of the four, including **EUG 125**, seen below on private hire duties, were rebuilt and rebodied using Eastern Coach Works 33-seat dual-purpose bodies taken from ex-United Automobile Services 1939 Leyland Tiger TS8s. EUG 126 was the one to retain its original Duple body. All were withdrawn between 1957 and 1959. *(Both: John Banks Collection)*

Here is a further comparison of the 1937 Leyland Tiger TS7s with original and with the Eastern Coach Works ex-United coachwork, in this case using images of the same vehicle, **EUG 124**. The upper view shows it emerging from Yeadon High Street. *(Both: John Fozard Collection)*

*Above:* Because of the link with Bradford through its ownership of B. & B. Tours Ltd, Ledgard vehicles were occasionally registered in that city. **BKW 909** was a 1937 Leyland Tiger TS7 with Duple 32-seat front-entrance coachwork, similar to EUG 124-7 of the same year already discussed and illustrated.

*Below:* A similar purchase the following year saw another Duple-bodied 32-seat Tiger TS7 join the fleet. **CKW 267** was again similar to vehicles (this time three: GUA 637-9) with Leeds registrations. *(Both: John Fozard Collection)*

The 1938 Duple-bodied Leyland Tiger TS7s were - as usual for that combination in that era - handsome, dignified vehicles. Here are two views of the middle of the three, **GUA 638**, photographed in Harrogate *(above)* and Otley bus station *(below)*. Along with GUA 639, this vehicle was withdrawn in 1957. GUA 637 had gone a year earlier, and their Bradford-registered sibling CKW 267 lasted two years longer, into 1959. GUA 637/8 ran again, albeit not in PSV service (they went to a travelling fairground showman and the building contractor Yorkshire Hennebique respectively); GUA 639 was scrapped without further use; CKW 267 ran for a builder and then a British Legion club and is believed to still exist in the United States. *(John Fozard Collection; Geoffrey Holt)*

# Wartime

*Above:* Delivered in 1940, after the outbreak of war, were three Leyland TD7 Titans, JNW 288-90, fitted with Leyland highbridge 56-seat bodywork. **JNW 289** was in King Street, Leeds, not long before its 1957 withdrawal. *(John Fozard Collection)*

*Below:* The Bedford OWB was a utility version of the late prewar OB model, in this case fitted with Roe utility 32-seat bodywork. **JNW 347** was one of a pair delivered at the height of the war in 1942. *(R F Mack Collection)*

*Above:* Wartime vehicle production was minutely controlled by two Government ministries: *Supply* and *War Transport*. Chassis and bodywork were built to a stern, utilitarian specification that precluded curves and any form of luxury. Guy Motors provided many of the chassis, including a pair to Ledgard in 1943. Fitted with Gardner 5LW engines they had Pickering, of Wishaw, Scotland, bodies. The second, **JUA 763**, is seen in the fifties after both had been fitted in 1951 with new Roe bodies and Gardner 6LW engines. In this condition they lasted in Ledgard service until 1961.

*Below:* Daimler was brought in later in the war as a utility chassis builder and in 1944 Ledgard was allocated four of the CWA6 (i.e. AEC 6-cylinder-engined) model, with Roe 56-seat highbridge bodywork. Eight similar chassis, plus two with Daimler engines (the CWD6 model) followed in 1945, this time all with Duple bodywork. **JUB 651** was one of the 1945 AEC-engined machines. *(Both: Geoffrey Holt)*

*Above:* Representing the Daimler-engined CWD6 models is **JUB 648** in Cookridge Street, Leeds. Its Duple body had been lightly modified with a rebuilt destination screen. Although supposedly to utility specification, the Daimlers had six-cylinder engines and preselector gearboxes and were thus smoother and easier to drive than the five-cylinder Guys with their crash gearboxes.

*Below:* Only an expert on the Ledgard fleet would know that this 1945 Daimler CWA6 was not all that it appeared. **JUB 649**, seen here in Otley bus station, had been rebodied in 1953 with a Park Royal body formerly carried by a London Transport Daimler. *(Both: Geoffrey Holt)*

# The Early Postwar Years

*Above:* After the war an unprecedented period of rationing and austerity lay ahead of the country; the bus builders (and the rest of manufacturing industry) were exhorted to export as much as they could - "Export or Die" was the slogan. By 1946, however, supplies of new buses were entering home fleets, including a batch of six highbridge all-Leyland PD1 56-seaters for Ledgard. Typical of them was **JUM 376**, seen at King Street, Leeds, in August 1949. All six were withdrawn between 1962 and 1965 - this one in 1964. *(G H F Atkins © John Banks Collection)*

*Below:* For its first postwar single-deckers, Ledgard remained faithful to the Leyland Tiger. By 1948 the model was the PS1 and six with Duple 33-seat half-cab coachwork were purchased, represented by **LUB 673** after conversion to fully fronted specification. *(R F Mack)*

*Upper:* A pair of similar 1948 Leyland Tiger PS1s, also Duple-bodied originally as 33-seaters, were registered in Bradford via the B. & B. Tours Ltd connection previously mentioned. **FAK 661/2** are represented by this shot of **FAK 662**. All eight of the 1948 PS1s were withdrawn in 1962/3. *(John Fozard Collection)*

*Centre:* The Leyland stranglehold on new vehicles for the Ledgard fleet was somewhat weakened in 1949/50 when six Foden PVSC6LW coaches were ordered. All were bodied as 33-seaters by Plaxton, four to half-cab layout, as on **MUA 864**, seen here in Leeds circa 1954. The other two were fully fronted. *(Geoffrey Holt)*

*Lower:* By 1949 the Leyland Titan had progressed to the more powerful PD2 model, and Ledgard took three of the PD2/1 variant, fitted with Leyland 56-seat highbridge bodies. Two of the three (MUA 860-2), led by **MUA 861**, show two variations on the Ledgard livery in King Street, Leeds, in about 1955. *(Geoffrey Holt)*

*Above:* The Foden theme continued in 1951 with **ONW 2**, a Plaxton-bodied fully fronted 37-seat coach. It was fitted with a Foden two-stroke diesel engine and survived to be taken over by West Yorkshire in 1967, though it was not used *(see also page 2). (Geoffrey Holt)*

*Below:* The Foden invasion did not extend to double-deckers for which Leyland was still the favoured supplier, and in 1952 three Titan PD2/12s were placed in service. The familiar 56-seat bodywork by Leyland was again specified. **PNW 93** is illustrated. *(R F Mack)*

# The Fifties Under the Executors

Samuel Ledgard's death in 1952 left his executors with no ordinary task in keeping the business on its feet and the blue buses running. There was no money for new buses in the quantities needed to replace the remaining prewar stock. Perhaps providentially, Samuel had kept large numbers of withdrawn vehicles on the premises, and these were sold for scrap and the money used to fund a fleet of utility Daimlers of which - again, providentially - London Transport wished to dispose. These vehicles were not wartime buses at all, having been delivered in 1946, and although undoubtedly "utility" in outward appearance, had been built to what has become known as the "relaxed utility"

style with more comprehensive destination screen layouts and more comfortable seating. No fewer than 23 of these far from time-expired Daimlers were acquired in 1953/4. As so often, the indefatigable Geoffrey Holt, at that time a resident of Leeds, was on hand, camera at the ready. These are his studies of **HGF 958** with original destination screens, and **HGF 891** with rebuilt screen more suited to Ledgard's requirements. *(Both: Geoffrey Holt)*

By 1955 matters were reasonably settled and a cautious return to ordering new vehicles was made. A lack of quality coaches was being felt, and six Burlingham Seagull bodies were ordered, three each with centre- or front- entrances and all 41-seaters. The chassis order was split between AEC (two Reliances) and Leyland (four Tiger Cubs). One of the Reliances, **UUA 791**, is seen as delivered *(above)* and as repainted in the lighter livery *(below)*. On the latter occasion it was at Wembley Stadium for a Harlem Globetrotters appearance. All six were taken into stock by West Yorkshire in 1967 but none was used. *(John Fozard Collection; Geoffrey Holt)*

*Above:* In 1956 a mixed bag of second-hand Daimlers (double- and single-deck), AECs and Leylands was acquired, including **FBU 896**, a 1950 Burlingham-bodied 33-seat Leyland PS2/3 coach, acquired from the operator Holts, of Oldham. It lasted eight years and was withdrawn in 1964.

*Below:* A superficially similar vehicle, **FBU 77** was a 1949 PS1 Tiger, with Plaxton coachwork, again seating 33. This one came from another Oldham area operator, Ralph Renton Ltd, of Hollinwood, and was withdrawn by Ledgard in 1960. *(Both: Geoffrey Holt)*

*Above:* Further variety from 1956 came with a pair of AEC Regal IIIs fitted with Beccols fully fronted 33-seat coachwork. JP 7865/8146 had been new to Smith, of Wigan, in 1949. They were both withdrawn in 1960. **JP 7865** is illustrated.

*Below:* Perhaps the most characterful of the 1956 selection was **LRW 377**, a Duple-bodied dual-entrance 36-seat service bus on a Daimler CD650H chassis. Formerly a demonstrator for Daimler, it was also scheduled for a short Ledgard career, going in 1960. It later ran for Bere Regis and District Motor Services, as did the AEC JP 7865. *(Both: Geoffrey Holt)*

New vehicles were again delivered in 1957, but this time the investment was in double-deck service buses. Seven were purchased and they introduced the concealed radiator styling arrangement (often referred to as "new look" or, somewhat dismissively, as "tin front") to the Ledgard fleet. Six of the seven comprised a batch of AEC Regent Vs of otherwise traditional rear-entrance, open-platform layout. The 65-seat bodywork was by Roe. The batch was registered 1949-54 U and all six survived to enter the West Yorkshire fleet in 1967, where they took WY fleet numbers DGW5-10. **1949 U** and **1950 U** are illustrated, the former (seen in Leeds) alongside one of that municipality's Daimlers by then running in the Ledgard fleet *(see pages 42/3)*.   *(Both: R F Mack)*

***Upper and centre:*** The other new look 1957 double-decker was **XUG 141**, a Daimler CVG6 with Burlingham 63-seat bodywork, seen here when brand new. This handsome bus also became a West Yorkshire vehicle in October 1967, with fleet number DGW12. *(John Banks Collection)*

***Lower:*** Daimler CWA6 **GHA 936** might have laid claim to the description "new look", too, after its original owner, Midland Red, had had its Weymann utility body rebuilt by Willowbrook in 1950. A 1943 vehicle, it was one of five bought from Midland Red by Ledgard in 1957. Perhaps the worst feature of the rebuild was the ugly, misaligned built-up front-nearside mudguard. The vehicle was withdrawn by Ledgard in 1962, the other five had gone in 1960/1. *(Geoffrey Holt)*

*Above:* The influx of second-hand half-cab coaches continued in 1957. **KUP 949** was a 1950 Leyland Tiger PS1 with 35-seat front-entrance coachwork by Burlingham, acquired from Baxter, of Airdrie. It passed to West Yorkshire in 1967 but was not used. It still exists in preservation. *(Geoffrey Holt)*

*Below:* **FJW 938** was rather more than it seemed at first glance. Using the chassis frames from a Birmingham Corporation AEC Regent, OG 373, Everall, of Wolverhampton, had built the vehicle in 1948 and had it bodied by Burlingham as a forward-entrance 33-seater. It was later in the fleet of Stubbs, of Stoke on Trent, before passing to Ledgard. *(John Fozard Collection)*

*Above:* The variety of second-hand acquisitions in 1957 included a former Guy Motors demonstrator in the shape of **GUY 3**, an appropriately registered 1951 Gardner six-cylinder-engined Guy Arab underfloor-engined service bus with 40-seat front-entrance body by Guy. It was in the fleet of Kitchin, of Pudsey, and was one of four vehicles to be transferred to Ledgard when Kitchin's routes were taken over in 1957. *(R F Mack)*

*Below:* A pair of Atkinson PL745H 44-seat service buses also came from Kitchin. Fitted with Burlingham front-entrance bodies, they dated from 1954. **NWW 806** was the second of them. Both were withdrawn in 1963. *(Geoffrey Holt)*

*Above:* Forward-engined chassis normally seen with half-cab bodies were not unknown with fully fronted coachwork: a sort of halfway stage between half-cabs and underfloor-engined coaches. A typical example was **JP 7221**, a Bellhouse-Hartwell-bodied Leyland PS1 33-seater, acquired from Smith, of Wigan. The chassis dated from 1948, and the body from 1952.

*Below:* As is often commented, the Duple Roadmaster was more popular as a Dinky Toy than as a real vehicle. The few that were built were functional but handsome, as demonstrated by **GVA 289**, a 1951 Leyland Royal Tiger ex-Baxter, of Airdrie. *(Both: Geoffrey Holt)*

In 1959 the intake was once more all of second-hand stock, including chassis of Albion, Bristol and Daimler manufacture. The solitary Daimler was **EN 8408**, a 1944 utility CWA6 chassis carrying a 1952 Roe 56-seat body, that had been No. 95 in the Bury Corporation fleet. It was withdrawn and sold for scrap in 1963. The photographs were taken at King Street, Leeds *(above)* and Lower Brook Street, Ilkley. *(Geoffrey Holt; John Fozard Collection)*

Albions with Tilling-style bodies were never common anywhere, and very few ran for independents. Ledgard bought five former Red and White CX13 model 35-seaters from a dealer in 1959, only to withdraw them in 1961/2. The chassis dated from 1946; the Bristol bodies were rather newer, having been fitted in 1951/2. The five were registered EWO 772/3, FAX 306/8/11, and are represented in Ledgard livery by **EWO 773** and **FAX 306**. (*Geoffrey Holt; John Fozard Collection*)

Five Eastern Coach Works-bodied Bristol double-deckers also appeared in 1959. There has been a suggestion that the executors had made approaches to West Yorkshire about selling the Company, and that hints had been made that the fleet ought to contain some vehicles familiar to West Yorkshire engineering staff. In any event, these five were acquired from United Automobile Services. They were all 1945 Bristol K6A (and therefore AEC-engined) chassis, with later (1949) bodies that they had received in 1954. **GHN 838** and **GHN 837** are illustrated. The other three were GHN 631/5, 840. They were withdrawn in 1964/5 and so never achieved re-entry into Tilling ownership. *(Ron Maybray Collection; R F Mack Collection/M H Lockyer)*

# The Last Decade

As the 1960s dawned enthusiasts could have been forgiven for thinking that Ledgard was an immutable part of the West Riding passenger transport scene: fiercely independent, eccentric and sometimes scruffy perhaps, but permanent. Those without inside knowledge could not have known about the difficulties and the dialogue with the West Yorkshire Road Car Company. For quite how long the writing was on the wall is not certain, but - despite the possible clue that lay in the flirtation with the products of Eastern Coach Works and Bristol - it came as a shock (this is John Banks writing) when in 1967 the announcement was made; the writer was taken to task by a friend for referring to it as "unbelievable" more or less in terms of "it is far from unbelievable to anyone with his eyes open". Well, be that as it may, the Executors managed to make the final years as interesting as any that had gone before with a continuing supply of second-hand and hired vehicles. The upper picture neatly sums up the fleet in those final years: second-hand Leyland Titans (**KHW 631** a PD1 ex-Bristol in 1961 and ECW-bodied; and PD2/12 **GTY 169**, with austere Metropolitan-Cammell Orion lightweight bodywork, ex-Tyneside in 1966) and ex-London Transport AEC Regents of the RT class represented here by **KXW 125**, acquired in 1965. In the picture on the right is another ex-Bristol Omnibus Company Titan PD1, **LAE 2**, a 1960 purchase. (*R F Mack; Geoffrey Holt*)

*Above:* It was quite an event when the first bus with a Bristol engine ran in service for a non-Tilling operator. It is believed that Ledgard's ex-Bristol Omnibus Company **KHU 603**, an ECW-bodied K6B lowbridge 55-seater was that notable first. It is seen at Otley bus station on 9th August 1962.

*Below:* No great journey was needed to deliver a batch of ten Brush-bodied Daimler CVD6s from Leeds Corporation to Ledgard in 1960. The batch, LNW 522-31, is represented by **LNW 531** in King Street, Leeds, on 10th April 1961. They dated from 1948, and four similar vehicles came from Exeter Corporation in the same year. *(Both: Philip Battersby)*

*Above:* The offside-front angle of the shapely Brush 56-seat rear-entrance bodywork of the ex-Leeds Daimlers is displayed on **LNW 524**. Some of Ledgard's other Daimlers had AEC or Gardner engines, but Daimler-engined versions had been in the fleet since 1944 *(see page 24)*. The Daimler engines in the ex-Leeds CVD6 models were thus not a new challenge for Ledgard's maintenance staff. *(Geoffrey Holt)*

*Below:* Most of the ex-Leeds Daimlers were withdrawn in 1963/4, only one - LNW 529 - surviving into 1965. Here are three of them - the first, last and one in between - **LNW 522/5/31**, giving some rare and interesting rear detail of the Brush bodywork. The picture was taken in Blamire's scrapyard, Bradford, on 4th April 1964. *(R F Mack Collection/M H Lockyer)*

Four Brush-bodied Daimler CVD6 56-seaters similar to the ex-Leeds machines had rather a longer journey to their new owner, although they did it via the premises of North, the Leeds dealer. JFJ 50-2/5 had been new to the Exeter Corporation fleet in 1948 and were almost exact contemporaries of the Leeds vehicles. **JFJ 55** and **JFJ 52** are illustrated, the latter taken at Otley bus station during the photographer's "take rear views of everything" phase. All four Exeter Daimlers were withdrawn in 1963. *(Geoffrey Holt; John Banks)*

*Above:* Second-hand coaches in 1960 included **KBU 880**, a Bedford SB with the familiar Duple coachwork, in this case seating 38. The vehicle had been new to an Oldham operator, and had come to Ledgard from subsequent owner Green, of Brierley Hill. It ran for Ledgard until 1963 and had at least three owners after withdrawal and sale to the dealer Hughes, of Gomersal. *(Geoffrey Holt)*

*Below:* Oldham registrations were a feature of the Ledgard fleet. Another two, GBU 537/9, appeared in 1960. They were Leyland PS2/3 Tigers with Plaxton 39-seat fully fronted coachwork, epitomised by **GBU 539**. Both were also withdrawn in 1963, the bodies scrapped and the chassis considered for rebodying by Ledgard, which in the event never happened. *(John Fozard Collection)*

*Above:* Another Daimler double-decker arrived in 1960. **SDU 711** was a CVG6 model with Willowbrook 66-seat rear-entrance bodywork fitted with platform doors. A 1956 vehicle, it had been a Daimler demonstrator and had appeared at the Commercial Motor Show in that year and again in 1958. It was photographed negotiating a roundabout at Otley Road, Leeds Ring Road, Weetwood on 25th April 1960. It ran for West Yorkshire after the takeover for two years. *(Philip Battersby)*

*Below:* By the early 1960s Leyland PD1 Titans of the immediate postwar period were becoming a little long in the tooth. Nonetheless, Ledgard bought some ex-Preston Corporation examples in 1961 and achieved reasonable service from them. **ARN 393** was one of the variant PD1A (the difference between that and a standard PD1 was a minor one connected with spring mounting) of which there were three, ARN 392-4. The vehicle passed to West Yorkshire but perhaps not surprisingly was not used. *(Bob Rowe)*

*Above:* As well as the three ARN-registered Titan PD1As, there were four BCK-registered examples from Ribble and four standard PD1s, also with BCK registrations, from Preston in 1961. **BCK 621** was one of the PD1s. The former Preston and Ribble Titans all had Leyland highbridge 56-seat bodies, reseated to 58 for Ledgard service. *(M H Lockyer)*

*Below:* A nice action shot of ex-Bristol **LAE 12**, a Leyland Titan PD1 with Eastern Coach Works 56-seat highbridge bodywork, at King Street and Wellington Street, Leeds, on 20th August 1962. This one was withdrawn in 1965 and used as a towing vehicle. *(Philip Battersby)*

*Above:* The writer in his "snap 'em from the back" mode again. Ex-Bristol Leyland Titan PD1 **KHW 243**, which had a Bristol body, was at Otley bus station. *(John Banks)*

*Below:* The Bristol bodywork again, shown off by **KHW 622**, another ex-Bristol Leyland Titan PD1. *(Geoffrey Holt)*

Among 1961's second-hand intake was another Bristol-engined vehicle. **KHY 746** was a standard Bristol K6B with highbridge 56-seat bodywork from the Lowestoft coach factory of Eastern Coach Works. *(Geoffrey Holt; M H Lockyer)*

*Above:* In 1962 began a considerable intake of AEC Regents. Most of them were to come from London Transport from 1963 onwards, but an interesting quintet of East Lancashire-bodied Regent III 59-seaters from Rochdale Corporation, including **GDK 404**, started the rush in 1962. They were withdrawn between 1965 and 1967, only one passing to West Yorkshire, who did not use it. *(R F Mack)*

Two more double-deckers in 1962 were a Leyland and an AEC from Felix, of Hatfield, Yorkshire. **JWU 131** (<< *opposite page lower*) was a 1950 Leyland-bodied 56-seat Titan PD2/1, and **GWY 157** (*this page*), a 1948 Regent III bodied, again as a 56-seater, by Roberts. Both trod the now familiar path of passing to West Yorkshire but not being used. Both were quickly sold for scrap. (*M H Lockyer; John Fozard Collection*)

The onslaught of ex-London vehicles began in 1963, of which more on later pages. That year was also notable for the arrival of a fleet of Picktree-bodied underfloor-engined Guy Arab LUF coaches. DCN 831/4-40 had been in the Northern General fleet and dated from 1954. A ninth, DCN 832, joined its stablemates in 1966 but was used only for spares. Our pictures are of **DCN 834** *(above)* and **DCN 839**. DCN 831 was used for spares by Ledgard; the other seven passed to West Yorkshire but saw no further use and were sold to North's; some of them ran again for building contractors as staff transport. *(Both: Geoffrey Holt)*

*Above:* The Ford 570E front-engined coach chassis was launched as a head-on challenge to Bedford's SB model. Both were lightweights, the type often favoured by independents, and both accepted virtually identical coachwork, usually seating 41, more often than not built by Duple or Plaxton. Ledgard bought two second hand year-old examples in 1963, of which we illustrate **252 BNW**, which was ex-Rodgers, a local Leeds operator. *(John Fozard Collection)*

*Below:* **MXX 176** was among the first, 1963, acquisitions of ex-London Transport RTs. It was photographed in Wellington Street, Leeds. *(M H Lockyer)*

*Above:* Among all the London RTs in 1963 was a solitary Leyland Titan. **EUH 959** was a PD2/3 model, carrying Leyland 53-seat lowbridge bodywork. It is seen at Yeadon depot in September 1966, alongside **KHU 602**. The Titan was ex-Samuel Eynon, of Trimsaran. *(M H Lockyer)*

*Below:* **KHU 602**, seen as a rear view in the picture above, had been in the Ledgard fleet since 1960. Although consecutively registered with KHU 603, the controversial Bristol-engined bus, KHU 602 was a Bristol K6A model, and thus AEC-engined. Senior management in the Tilling organisation worried less about such engines "escaping". *(John Fozard Collection/Geoffrey Holt)*

Operating coaches has ever been a highly competitive, not to say cut-throat, business, and the operator who fields old, down-at-heel vehicles runs the risk of seeing his customers go elsewhere with their private hire work. There was a constant need for the Executors to address this problem and in 1964 a solution was found through the hire of six Bedford SB5s from the dealer Hughes, of Gomersal. All were 41-seaters, four bodied by Plaxton and two, of which we illustrate **846 HUA**, by Duple. All were returned to Hughes (across the years 1964-7) and all went on to serve subsequent owners. *(Both: Senior Transport Archive)*

*Above:* More ex-Ribble Leyland Titans came in 1964 in the shape of four Titan PD2/3s with Leyland lowbridge 53-seat bodywork, the last of which (DRN 273) had platform doors. One of the three open-platform versions, **CRN 855** (the other two were CRN 852/66) is seen at Buckle Lane in April 1967.

*Below:* The influx of dozens of ex-London Transport RTs during the last four years of the Company's existence produced many scenes such as this one inside Otley depot in February 1964. Recent arrival **LYR 918** (ex-RT3499) was being prepared for Ledgard service - a far cry from the vehicle's erstwhile maintenance surroundings at Aldenham Works. *(Both: M H Lockyer)*

*Above:* The coach-hiring exercise was repeated in 1965 when two new Plaxton-bodied Leyland Leopard PSU3/3R models (as well as a second-hand Bedford SB1) were hired from Hughes. The 51-seat Leylands were still in service when the Company was sold to West Yorkshire and were returned to Hughes. **AUM 414C** was photographed outside Otley depot in April 1965.

*Below:* Ex-London Transport RTL305 (**KGU 263**) is seen here in Ledgard ownership but in Halifax, well out of Ledgard territory, on private hire work. It had a busy career after sale from London in 1959 and was well known for its use in the Silver Star, of Porton Down, fleet. In 1965 it was bought by the Executors and survived to pass to West Yorkshire, once again without being used. It was preserved but lost its body in a fire and the chassis was eventually scrapped. *(Both: M H Lockyer)*

Although there never was a lowbridge RT, London came quite close to the idea with the RLH class, which was the provincial version of the AEC Regent III with standard Weymann, of Addlestone, 53-seat bodywork. When they came onto the second-hand market Ledgard bought four, all with KYY registrations (KYY 502/4/6/8), in 1964/5. West Yorkshire became the owner of this quartet - as it did of lots of Ledgard ex-London RTs - in October 1967, but never used them. **KYY 502** ended up back in London Transport livery for service in the United States of America. Both these photographs were taken at Yeadon depot. *(M H Lockyer; R F Mack)*

*Above:* By 1966 there was perhaps a hint of desperation evident in the Executors' second-hand purchases, which included 19-year-old (albeit modernised) ex-Ribble PD1As and a variety of AECs and other Leylands, none less than eleven years old. **PDV 732** was one of a pair of ex-Devon General AEC Regent IIIs with Weymann 58-seat rear-entrance bodywork with platform doors. *(M H Lockyer)*

*Below:* Among the 1966 Leyland Titan input were four ex-London Transport RTLs. These 7RT models (which were substantially modified PD2s) had Metro-Cammell bodywork and - though in the minority among the ex-London stock - added some relief to the parade of AECs. *(R F Mack)*

*Above:* The ex-Ribble Leyland Titans, BCK 427/41, had been new in 1947 as PD1A models and were rebodied by Burlingham in 1955 as platform-door lowbridge 53-seaters. In 1958 a further upgrading saw Leyland O.600 engines fitted. **BCK 427** was outside Bradford depot in 1967. *(John Fozard Collection/M H Lockyer)*

*Below:* **GTY 169** was a 1954 Leyland Titan PD2/12 with the ungainly and utilitarian lightweight Orion bodywork from Metro-Cammell. It had been new to the Tyneside fleet and was a 58-seater. *(R F Mack)*

## 1967 - The Final Year

*Above:* There had been two ex-South Wales Weymann-bodied AEC Regent Vs in 1966, and the following year another pair appeared. NCY 453/5 (and 1966's MCY 405/8) passed, like much else, to West Yorkshire but in this case were actually used. The vehicle illustrated, **NCY 453**, became WY DAW3 and ran until October 1969. *(M H Lockyer)*

*Below:* The by now regular coach hiring from Hughes produced four Plaxton-bodied Bedford VAM14s in 1967, exemplified by **JUB 304E**. All went back to Hughes in October of that year. *(John Fozard Collection)*

So what was it that caused the Ledgard fleet to attract such a loyal following? And such sadness when it disappeared into the vastness of the Transport Holding Company? It was independent, to start with, and was by some perceived as David fighting the Goliath of the big company operators. Then there was its vehicle policy, which produced fine new buses and coaches cheek-by-jowl with a fascinating selection of second-hand vehicles from all over the place - although on a smaller scale, one is reminded of the Barton fleet. In the later years, before the October 1967 sell-out to West Yorkshire, there was no doubt that the "second-hand" image predominated, and at that in quite separate strands - two of which were ex-London RTs and ex-Tilling Bristols. These views at Otley bus station on different days in the summer of 1964 show both, in the shape of **LYR 926** and **LHU 520** making dramatic exits on the way to Leeds. But...

*M H Lockyer*

... maybe, in the end, the picture that the mind's eye most often conjures up on hearing the word "Ledgard" is of Leyland-bodied Titans with exposed radiators. New or second-hand, PD1 or PD2, once in Sammy's blue livery they came to epitomise a much-loved, if somewhat eccentric, operator, now gone for almost four decades.